PENGUINS

Wildlife Monographs – Penguins
Copyright ©2006 Evans Mitchell Books

Text and Photography Copyright ©2006 Fritz Pölking

Fritz Pölking has asserted his rights to be identified as
the author and photographer of this work in
accordance with Section 77 of the Copyright, Designs
and Patents Act 1988

First published in the United Kingdom by:
Evans Mitchell Books
Norfolk Court, 1 Norfolk Road,
Rickmansworth, Hertfordshire WD3 1LA
United Kingdom

Jacket and Book Design by:
Roy Platten
Eclipse
roy.eclipse@btopenworld.com

Translated from the original German by Julian Wagstaff
Edited by Maggie Stanfield

British Library Cataloguing in Publication Data.
A CIP record of this book is available on request
from the British Library.

ISBN: 1-901268-14-4

Pre Press: F.E Burman, London, United Kingdom

Printed in Thailand

PENGUINS

FRITZ PÖLKING

Evans Mitchell Books

Contents

Introduction

Why do they do that? Emperor penguins are known to breed when it's dark for nearly 24 hours each day, when the temperature hits lows of minus 40° Celsius, in the midst of storms which are – literally – unbearable. They balance incubating eggs on their feet to keep them from touching the ice beneath. Why do they do that?

Perhaps it's because all life on earth originated in ice. Researchers have recently discovered that so-called ribonucleic acid (RNA) – the substance which seems to have played a central role in the emergence of life on earth – abounds in ice floes.

Under certain circumstances these molecules are able to reproduce by themselves, and this is believed to have been an important step on the path to life. This is said to have occurred 3.8 billion years ago in the eternal ice of the Antarctic.

Above: A pretty picture of strolling emperor penguins – an archetype of penguins in tailcoats.

Right: Emperor penguins in a snowstorm on the Dawson-Lambton Glacier.

If this is true, then it's possible to construct a theory that life began in the Antarctic, and that the penguins simply remained there. It's certainly a nice theory…

Birds began to emerge around 200 million years ago, and were so successful that they were able to establish themselves right across the globe – evolving by degrees into 27 orders, around 200 families and such a vast number of different species that, even now, not all of them are known to us.

Among them, penguins constitute a single family in a single order, and their 17 species all look more or less the same.

At some point in the past they could certainly fly, but they have since given up this ability in favour of being able to swim (or fly) better under water.

Penguins have adapted more perfectly to a life in and under the water than any other family of birds. They regularly reach top speeds of 25 km/h and can dive continuously for over 15 minutes, and to incredible depths of over 500 metres, depending on the species. The larger, the faster; the longer, the deeper.

Penguins are among the best known and best loved of all birds, and they don't exist only in and around Antarctica – contrary to popular belief. The fact that they also live and breed in Africa, Australia and America is not so well known, in spite of their undoubted popularity around the world.

Opposite page: A young king penguin looks fatter than its parents.

Overleaf: In the first few weeks, the emperor penguins carry their young on their hands – metaphorically speaking. In fact they carry them on their feet.

History and Distribution

While birds as a type began to emerge around 200 million years ago, penguins only began to appear around 45 to 65 million years ago. They are assumed to have had their origins in New Zealand. Almost all of the 32 species of penguin which are now extinct were identified in New Zealand and Australia.

We mustn't forget that three million years ago there were still forests in Antarctica.

Of those extinct species, one startling example was between 1.5 and 1.6 metres tall (pachydyptes ponderosus) and lived from the Oligocene era 38 million years ago until the early Miocene era 25 million years ago.

Most species of birds have been able to fly since around 100 million years ago, but for a long time it was not clear whether penguins were descended from birds which could fly at all. Now, it seems fairly clear that they are.

Detailed investigations by scientists have led them to the conclusion that the non-flying penguin is closely related to the storm petrel and the albatross, and not to the great auk, which became extinct on 3rd July 1844.

Left: A rookery (colony) of Macaroni penguins in Hercules Bay on South Georgia. Contrary to the clichéd image, most penguins do not live on 'eternal ice'.

Above: King penguin chicks.

Penguin Habitats

Antarctica
Emperor penguin
Adelie penguin

Antarctic Peninsula
Chinstrap penguin
Gentoo penguin

Subantarctic Islands
King penguin
Royal penguin
Rockhopper penguin
Macaroni penguin
Gentoo penguin

South Africa
African penguin

Australia, New Zealand
Yellow-eyed penguin
Erect-crested penguin
Fiordland penguin
Snares penguin
Little blue penguin (fairy penguin)
White-flippered penguin

South America
Magellanic penguin
Humboldt penguin
Gentoo penguin (Falkland Islands)
Rockhopper penguin (Falkland Islands)

Galapagos Islands
Galapagos penguin

Opposite page, top: Emperor penguins in Antarctica

Opposite page, bottom: King penguins prefer things a little warmer: Here is a colony of them on the Falkland Islands.

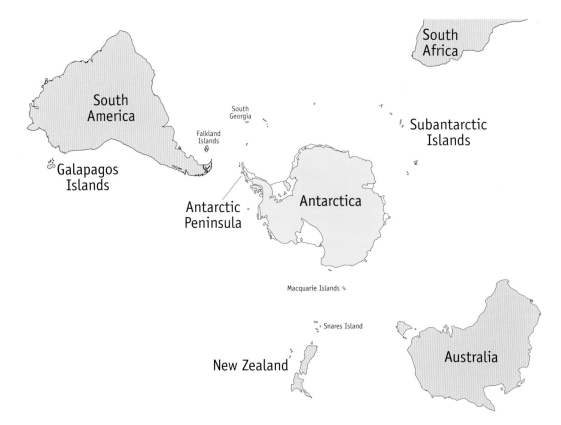

South Africa

South America

Falkland Islands

South Georgia

Subantarctic Islands

Galapagos Islands

Antarctic Peninsula

Antarctica

Macquarie Islands

Snares Island

New Zealand

Australia

Distinguishing Features

Penguins have highly streamlined bodies, which are perfectly suited to a life in and under the water. This frame means that penguins are extremely fast and use up very little energy in the water. However, their wings are too short for flying. Scientists have calculated that a penguin would have to reach a ground speed of around 400 km/h before it would be able to take off into the air. For this reason they can only 'fly' under water!

Penguin feathers are 3 cm long, and each square centimetre of a penguin's skin is covered by 12 feathers. Just above the skin, the feathers form a dense forest of eiderdown – a kind of 'thermal underwear'. They can swim and dive like dolphins, and their short wings, covered in little feathers, are mainly used for swimming.

The fact that they look black when seen from above and white from below is an aid to camouflage. Seen from above, you can hardly tell them from the dark ocean beneath them, and from below they look just like the bright surface of the water.

Left: Gentoo penguins enjoy a heated discussion on a beach in the Falkland Islands

Above: The golden crest of Macaroni penguins make them very easy to recognise.

Penguins are the easiest to describe of all bird species: "They're white at the front, black at the back, and walk like a waiter in a tailcoat."

Serious scientific descriptions are relatively recent:

1758   Carl von Linne described the African and the rockhopper penguin.

1768   Thomas Pennant described the king penguin

1776   Pierre Sonnerat described the gentoo and the Magellanic penguin.

1837   Johann Friedrich Brandt described the Macaroni penguin.

1841   Jacques-Bernand Hombron and Charles Hector Jacquinot described the adelie and the yellow-eyedpenguin.

1844   George Robert Gray described the Fiordland and the emperor penguin.

Opposite page: In return for payment in the form of a few fish, penguins in the Antarctic are sometimes used as landing guides on airstrips. That's why they've got these yellow headsets, familiar in all of the world's airports, but here in the Antarctic they have an additional function as insulation against the cold – as demonstrated by this king penguin.

The number of known species of penguin still with us is generally reckoned to be 17, although this figure is somewhat contentious. There are some scientists who count only 15 separate species, while others claim that there are 22, because it is debateable whether some of the sub-species are in fact species in their own right. Here are the six genera of penguin, with a total of 17 species:

Genus Aptenodytes
Emperor penguin
King penguin

Genus Pygoscelis
Adelie penguin
Chinstrap penguin
Gentoo penguin

Genus Megadyptes
Yellow-eyed penguin

Genus Spheniscus
Magellanic penguin
Humboldt penguin
Galapagos penguin
African penguin

Genus Eudyptes
Macaroni penguin
Royal penguin
Rockhopper penguin
Erect-crested penguin
Fiordland penguin
Snares penguin

Genus Eudyptula
Little blue penguin (fairy penguin)

Habitat and Diet

There are penguins in Australia, Africa, America and Antarctica. Why, then, are there no penguins in the Arctic? Why is it only possible to produce a photograph of a polar bear with a penguin on a computer using photography software and not with a camera alone?

The habitats may be similar and may even look the same to us. If penguins can swim as far as the Galapagos Islands, then why can't they manage it just a little bit further – to Alaska for example?

It probably has something to do with the carnivores that inhabit the northern hemisphere, such as foxes, lynx, wolves, stoats and polar bears. But the great auk managed it nonetheless. It was human beings that finally made that creature extinct. Perhaps it was the warm water currents in the temperate zones which prevented the penguin from conquering the Arctic.

Penguins have a body temperature of 39 degrees centigrade, the same as our own.

Opposite page: The food source.

Above: Tussac grass on the Falkland Islands. Another biotope where penguins can be found.

They can easily survive water temperatures anywhere between minus 40°C and minus 1°C because of the excellent insulation provided by their feather coats and the fat layer under their skin.

For this reason they have no problem catching their food in cold water – shoalfish, cuttlefish or krill. They swim by zig-zagging into a shoal of fish and catching as many of them as they can manage to.

Since the cool waters of their home territories are so very rich in potential food, they can easily catch the huge quantities of fish that a large rookery needs to survive and to rear the young into adulthood. A thousand large penguins need around a tonne of food per day, and a large penguin can eat and digest up to 10 kg of fish on a single foray.

These forays take place at various depths. The deepest that a little blue penguin can dive is 30 metres. African penguins can dive to 140 metres, king penguins up to 325 meters, and emperor penguins as deep as 535 metres.

Penguins are believed to find their way back to the breeding colony using the position of the sun and the stars.

Above: King penguins heading for their element.

Opposite page, top: Penguins live and breed here on the Galapagos islands, although we won't be seeing ice and snow here for at least another 10,000 years.

Opposite page, bottom: This is how we imagine the life of a penguin: adrift on an ice floe.

Overleaf: A giant breeding colony of king penguins on South Georgia.

Social Structure and Communication

Penguins do have ears, although they are well hidden under feathers. They communicate by trumpeting, moaning, squealing and growling. Individual animals can be recognised by their calls even in large rookeries. Research shows that penguins almost always return to the same partner and nesting site each year. Between mating seasons, they live separately at sea, so they must find one another again first.

About half of all first-time brooding penguins do so in the colony in which they were born. The rest migrate to distant locations.

The chance of successful breeding increases with age and experience. The offspring, too, have better survival rates. Penguins start breeding anywhere between the ages of two and six years depending on species.

Social life is usually within large groups. Penguins construct countless numbers of little groups, larger groups and huddles. This is perhaps also a reason for the complicated love life of penguins. For example, the 'oldest

Opposite page: A gentoo penguin gets itself noticed.

Above: Young penguins are often seen together in nurseries.

27

profession on earth' is also known in the penguin world. Researchers at the universities of Cambridge (England) and Otago (New Zealand) have filmed female penguins in the Antarctic 'hustling' for clients.

The females hire themselves for amorous services in return for small pebbles. This unit of currency is the most precious thing there is in the penguin world because the pebbles are needed for building nests and are very difficult to find.

These females have not found themselves lovers but have simply sold themselves for sex. Since penguins have been around for many millions of years longer than humans, the history of prostitution may have to be largely re-written!

Below: Penguins often walk in large or small social groups.

Opposite page, top: Social cohesion is particularly striking in the larger penguin species.

Opposite page, bottom: It is hard to imagine a more close-knit social fabric.

Overleaf: Some female birds will go on the 'penguin strip' for pebbles like these.

Reproduction

Penguins live amid ice and snow. Most of them also live under the tropical sun, but always within range of cold ocean currents. At breeding time they head for land to mate, almost always with the same partner, and to bring up their young.

After the couple have found a suitable site, they begin to build their nest. Emperor and king penguins save themselves some work here, because they hatch their young on their feet and the egg lies in a pouch on the stomach. The reason for this is probably that there is hardly any nesting material to be found in these species' breeding grounds. Even the young penguin is carried around in this brood pouch above the feet until it grows too big.

The adelie, gentoo and chinstrap penguins build their nests from little pebbles. African, little blue, humboldt, magellanic and galapagos penguins incubate in caves and holes, while other species build there nests from branches and blades of grass.

The eggs are laid a few days after the balancing act which is penguin mating. Emperor and king penguins lay one egg; the other species usually lay two eggs at the most.

The incubation period lasts between one and two months. The general rule applies to all – the larger the penguin, the longer the egg takes to hatch.

Above: Skuas are aggressive birds who profit from the penguin breeding cycle. Here, they have plundered rockhopper penguin eggs.

Opposite page: A king penguin feeds its large chick.

Overleaf: This gentoo penguin has found a quite exquisite nesting place for itself: among the bones of a dead whale.

The Headless Baron Penguin

On 1st April 1936, the well-known penguin researcher Prof. Dr Mattias Landscheiten from Vorst in Germany discovered a new species of penguin, the headless baron penguin (Aptenodytes baronu), in a remote part of Salisbury Plain on South Georgia.

Of course, it isn't really headless, but it can draw its head in – probably as a way of adapting to the harsh climate and the viciously cold winters.

Probably because of its position in between the two other large penguins, the king penguin and the emperor penguin, the penguin was named the baron penguin.

As you can see from the picture of the two brown baby birds, this penguin is not just a chance cross-breed, but is capable of reproducing. This species is said to have emerged around 250,000 years ago.

Growing Up

The road to independence is of varying lengths for different species of young penguins. King penguins babies may need up to 12 months, while adelie penguins manage it in only 45 days. Most others species take between two and three months.

The offspring of emperor penguins, king penguins and a few other species are raised grouped together in 'nurseries'. This arrangement provides them with good protection against the cold and also against predators such as harriers. Within the groups, the chicks are fed individually by their own parents.

The familiar feather coat only appears on the young penguins after the first year of life, when they finish moulting.

Only when protected by their real feathers do the young penguins head for the sea. By this time, the children have left their parents long ago and must learn to swim, dive and hunt for prey entirely on their own.

Oposite page: A highly emotive image from the world of the emperor penguin.

Above: The young emperor penguins snuggle up to one another when the wind and the ferocious cold make it advisable.

Penguins of the World

Order: *Sphenisciformes*
Family: *Spheniscidae*

Penguins are the only birds among all the orders which have just a single family. They are also the only birds who have opted for a life in the water; not to swim on top of the water like many other species of bird, but to swim in it instead.

They have paid a price for their accomplished swimming ability, however, in sacrificing their ability to fly. But by doing so they became the most perfectly adapted sea-creatures of all birds.

When it comes to species of penguin, there is still no complete unity among the experts about what constitutes a genus and what constitutes a sub-species. In this book, we have worked on the basis of 17 species, though many writers count 22, including the sub-species.

The reason behind the ongoing debate is the genetic isolation of some groups or populations. Over the course of time, some of the groups have formed into new species via intermediate stages – but always in a fluid transition.

Opposite page: On the Galapagos Islands, penguins co-exist alongside marine iguanas and gannets.

Above: Adelie penguins on the Antarctic Peninsula. A more intimate picture.

Overleaf: Gentoo penguins on the Antartica Peninsula.

Emperor Penguin

Genus:	*Aptenodytes*
Species:	*Aptenodytes forsteri*
Population:	circa 200,000 pairs
Status:	stable
Height:	circa 100 – 130 cm
Weight:	23 – 40 kg
Food:	fish
Breeding grounds:	the pack ice belt around the Antarctic continent.

The emperor penguin is the largest of all penguins and, alongside the adelie penguin, the species with the most southerly distribution. It is perhaps the only penguin which virtually never comes into contact with land, and is the best adapted to the cold. On land, it has an upright gait, and it does not build nests. Firstly the egg, and later the chicks, are carried on the penguin's feet and protected in a pouch.

It lays its egg between July and September when the climate is at its coldest and darkest and temperatures are as low as minus 40 to minus 60 degrees centigrade. The breeding adult birds huddle together to resist the cold and minimise their heat loss. Penguins breed early because the young are not independent until at least the age of six months – that is, at the time of the Antarctic spring.

At the time of writing, there are 42 known emperor penguin breeding colonies. The groups move around and have been seen around South Georgia and the Falkland Islands, for example, although they do not generally come onto land.

They are probably the most familiar of penguins and their young are certainly the most endearing from a human perspective. At first glance they look similar to the king penguin, but in fact differ on account of their size and the different colouring on the neck and gullet.

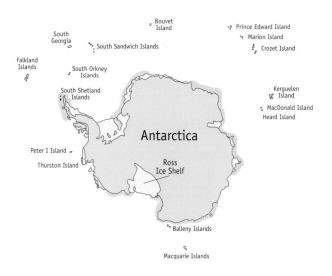

King Penguin

Genus: *Aptenodytes*
Species: *Aptenodytes patagonicus*
Population: over one million pairs
Status: stable
Height: circa 75 – 100 cm
Weight: circa 10 – 20 kg
Food: fish
Breeding grounds: Antarctic and Sub-Antarctic islands.

The king penguin looks similar to the emperor penguin, but is smaller. In addition, the colouring around the head and neck is different, and it has no feathering at the base of its lower bill.

The king penguin is the second largest species of penguin and, in a manner of speaking, is the sub-Antarctic version of the large emperor penguin. It also resembles its larger cousin in the way it builds its nest: that is, it doesn't build any nest at all! King penguins are not as tolerant within the breeding colony and keep a greater distance from their neighbours than do the emperor penguins.

King penguins breed in the southern oceans from the Tierra del Fuego to the Macquarie Islands, and also on the Falkland Islands. They have an upright gait and do not hop. They carry their single eggs on their feet in the same way as the emperor penguin, covered by a fold of skin or pouch.

They have an irregular breeding cycle, breeding twice every three years or only once every two years, because their young grow up very slowly. The complete breeding cycle on South Georgia, for example, is 14 months. The incubation period for the egg is 54 – 55 days and the young take 11 – 12 months to grow up.

They migrate as far as New Zealand, Australia, South Africa and South America.

Gentoo Penguin

Genus:	*Pygoscelis*
Species:	*Pygoscelis papua*
Population:	circa 320,000 pairs
Status:	stable
Height:	circa 80 cm
Weight:	6 – 7 kg
Food:	fish, krill
Breeding grounds:	coasts around the Antarctic continent, sub-Antarctic islands, circum-polar regions.

The gentoo penguin is coloured slate-grey on its upper side and brownish-black on its neck, gullet and head. The young birds look similar to their parents but have brownish-black flecks on their gullets and chins.

The gentoo penguin has the widest distribution of all penguin species. One place you won't find them is Papua New Guinea, the place where they get their name. They are to be found in the southern oceans from Antarctica up to New Zealand and Tasmania. They often remain close to their breeding grounds for the entire year and are much more peaceable than other penguin species.

The nick-name 'rockhopper' is often used for this species, even though they don't hop when on land, but in fact run. You may also hear them called 'Johnny' penguins.

The breeding season begins in September with the establishment of rookeries and the building of nests. Normally, gentoo penguins lay two eggs. The young are ready in January and go into the sea in February or March. Lobster krill, along with squid and schooling fish are also important sources of food.

Adelie Penguin

Genus:	*Pygoscelis*
Species:	*Ppygoscelis adeliae*
Population:	circa 2.5 million pairs.
Status:	stable
Height:	circa 70 – 75 cm.
Weight:	3 – 6 kg
Food:	krill
Breeding grounds:	on the coasts of the Antarctic and the surrounding islands.

The adelie penguin is coloured blue-black on its upper side and pure black on its upper head, cheeks and gullet. These penguins have short, brick-red bills with feet which are pinkish-white on top and black on the bottom. Their young look similar, but have bills which are white, like their undersides, and black eyelids and blackish bills.

Adelie penguins were, for many decades, considered to be the most common species of penguin. However, accurate censuses have shown that there are in fact more macaroni and chinstrap penguins than there are adelie penguins.

In winter adelie are to be found in pack-ice regions and during the breeding season, around the coasts of the Antarctic and its surrounding islands.

Because the adelie penguin only needs three months to incubate, they begin the process much later in the year than do the emperor penguins. They spend most of the year at sea along the northern corner of the pack-ice.

They take their name from the wife of the man who discovered them, who was called Adélie.

The adelie penguin walks in a particularly upright fashion, moving slowly and waddling.

In the snow and ice they like to slide along on their chests, using their wings and feet to propel themselves forward. When they swim in the water, their backs are underneath the surface.

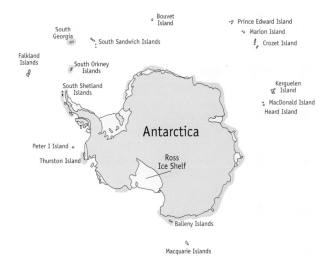

Magellanic Penguin

Genus: *Spheniscus*
Species: *Spheniscus magellanicus*
Population: 750,000 – 2 million pairs
Status: stable
Height: circa 70 – 76 cm
Weight: between 2.8 – 5 kg
Food: fish
Breeding grounds: along the southern coasts of South America.

Megellanic penguins look similar to humboldt penguins but have an additional black band on the front of their necks. Magellanic young resemble their parents but their gullets are dark grey as is a broad band along the front of their necks.

They lay their eggs between October and December and breed along the coasts of South America from Patagonia to southern Chile. They usually return to their breeding grounds in September and breed there from mid-October.

Their nests are found in hollows in the ground, between bushes and rocks. After about 38 – 41 days the young hatch and leave their holes around the end of January. Their food is usually schooling fish and squid.

Their donkey-like calls are similar to those of the African penguins of the Cape of Good Hope.

In winter, the birds from the Pacific coast head towards Peru, and those of the Atlantic coast head for Brazil. One-year-old chicks return in December/January to the breeding site at which they were born.

On the Falkland Islands, too, they are widespread on all of the islands which have tussac grass, where they like to build their nest holes. In some areas they also incubate above ground.

Like all penguins breeding in temperate zones, they are exposed to man-made dangers such as oil deposits on the ocean or stray drift nets.

Galapagos Islands

South America

Falkland Islands

Chinstrap Penguin
(Bearded Penguin)

Genus:	*Pygoscelis*
Species:	*Pygoscelis antarctica*
Population:	circa 7.5 million pairs.
Status:	stable
Height:	circa 72 – 78 cm.
Weight:	3.9 – 5.4 kg.
Food:	krill
Breeding grounds:	South Atlantic Ocean to the Antarctic Peninsula.

The chinstrap penguin is blue-grey when seen from above, with a blackish upper head and white on its gullet, neck and underside. It has a striking black line above its gullet from one ear to the other, which makes it practically impossible to mistake.

Its lower wings are white, with a black fleck at the tip and a black outer rim. They are much more aggressive than the other two species of the same genus.

Chinstrap penguins often go on the offensive when other species would take flight. They are said to be the second most common species of penguin, though the estimate of 7.5 million breeding pairs is not entirely without contention.

They live in the southern Atlantic Ocean and the Antarctic Ocean. In winter, they are to be seen as far afield as the Falkland Islands and in the east as far as the longitude 106° East. Their breeding colonies can be very large. Most pairs breed on the South Sandwich Islands, where around five million pairs live in rookeries.

Laying time is between October and February. They are at sea from May to September. Their numbers appear to be stable or may even have increased slightly as a result of the warming of the southern oceans. For this reason, too, their distribution seems to be greatly increasing.

They are often also known as 'ring' penguins, because of their white chin and the narrow black line which appears above the gullet.

Photos: Winfried Wisniewski

African Penguin
(Jackass or Black-footed Penguin)

Genus:	*Spheniscus*
Species:	*Spheniscus demersus*
Population:	circa 80,000
Status:	under threat; almost at risk of extinction
Height:	circa 64 – 69 cm
Weight:	4.0 – 4.3 kg
Food:	fish
Breeding grounds:	The coasts of South Africa.

The African penguin has a black crown, front, gullet and upper side. Its underside is white, with a black stripe above its chest and along the sides of its body down to its flanks. A white stripe runs from the base of its bill, over the sides of its crown and neck, down to the flanks above the black stripe. It has a white speck on its tail and its wings are black on top with white stripes on either side.

The African penguin is a home-loving bird and remains in the same area as its breeding ground more often than other species of penguin. It ventures up to 10 kilometres away from the coast in search of food. Young African penguins, on the other hand, can travel many hundreds of kilometres away from their rookery.

There are many busy shipping routes along the coasts of South Africa. As a result, and because their eggs are being collected under the supervision of the government, African penguin numbers have reduced catastrophically.
In 1900, half a million pairs used to breed there. Now the number of extant pairs is estimated to be 80,000.

This is the only kind of penguin to be found on the African coast and the breeding season continues virtually the whole year round, with May-June being the busiest months. The rookeries are to be found on the mainland and on the neighbouring islands.

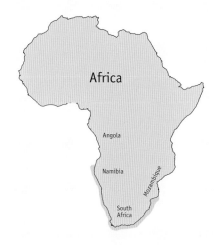

Photos: Grover Larkins

Galapagos Penguin

Genus: *Spheniscus*
Species: *Spheniscus mendiculus*
Population: circa 3000 – 10,000 birds
Status: endangered
Height: circa 50 – 53 cm
Weight: circa 1.7 – 2.5 kg
Food: small fish
Breeding grounds: Galapagos Islands

The galapagos penguin looks similar to the magellanic penguin but is substantially smaller. Its chin and its forward gullet are white with a small stripe and a white band along the neck and crown. Its wings are slate-coloured, black beneath, with a wide stripe as far as the centre and white speckling on the inner edge.

The galapagos penguin is one of the smallest of all penguins, and is the only one which is specifically tropical. The temperatures on the Galapagos Islands can easily rise to 40 degrees celsius.

These penguins live the whole year round on the Islands and are usually to be encountered on Fernandina and on the western and northern coasts of Isabela.

Here, they search for food in the cold and food-rich Humboldt stream. It is practically impossible to mistake them for any other species because they are endemic to the Galapagos Islands so they can only be found here and indeed are the only species of penguin on these islands.

The severe and very long-lasting El Niño disruption of the ocean-atmosphere system between 1982 and 1984 saw the population decimated by around 80%. Since then, the species has slowly recovered from this catastrophic slump.

Humboldt Penguin

Genus: *Spheniscus*
Species: *Spheniscus humboldti*
Population: fewer than 5000 pairs.
Status: under threat; almost at risk of extinction
Height: circa 65 – 73 cm.
Weight: 5 – 5.5 kg
Food: fish
Breeding grounds: West coast of South America from Chile to Peru.

The humboldt penguin is brownish-grey or slate-grey on its upper side. The sides of its head and throat are blackish. Its chin and a stripe from its beak along the sides of its crown and down the side of its neck are white. Its neck at the front and the underside of the bird are also white. It also has a distinctive dark band which runs in a horseshoe shape over its chest to its tail.

This penguin gets its name from the Humboldt stream which moves along the western coast of South America. That stream is almost certainly also responsible for the fact that penguins were able to extend their area of distribution as far as the Galapagos Islands and that the species of Galapagos penguin was able to emerge at all.

The breeding grounds of the humbolt and magellanic penguins overlap along a stretch of coast of between 250 and 300 miles long. They often build their nests in old guano – seabird excrement – deposits. Guano depletion, over-fishing of the Humboldt Stream and oil pollution are affecting these birds very badly.

As a source of guano, humboldts were previously very important. Since they thrive very well in zoos and also reproduce there, breeding programmes are concentrating on this species in particular. They breed on the coast and on offshore islands and lay their eggs at any time of the year. Humboldt penguins stay near to their breeding colony for the entire year.

Photos: Fred Bruemmer (Okapia)

Macaroni Penguin

Genus: *Eudyptes*
Species: *Eudyptes chrysolophus*
Population: circa 12 million pairs
Status: stable
Height: circa 65 – 77 cm.
Weight: 3.4 – 6.1 kg.
Food: krill
Breeding grounds: Antarctic Peninsula, southern Atlantic and Indian Ocean.

The macaroni penguin has a dark blue-grey upper side with a blackish chin, head and throat. The golden feathers above its forehead give it its characteristic appearance and the reason for its German name which means 'gold-crested penguin.' This decorative headgear makes it look particularly attractive and friendly to human eyes. The golden crest is its trademark, its branding if you like.

Macaronis often breed close to rockhopper penguins, but around two weeks later in the year.

They seem to be the most common type of penguin, and their large breeding colonies are found on South Georgia, the Crozet Islands, the Kerguelen, Heard and Macquarie Islands, with around five million breeding pairs on each.

The birds come to the breeding sites in October, incubate between November and January and leave the rookeries in April or May.

Macaroni penguins feed on lobster, krill and small fish.

They can be distinguished from the erect-crested, rockhopper and fiordland penguin by the colouring of the lines on the side of their crowns, and from the royal penguin by their dark-coloured throats.

Royal Penguin

Genus: *Eudyptes*
Species: *Eudyptes schlegeli*
Population: circa 850,000 pairs
Status: stable
Height: circa 70 – 75 cm
Weight: 4.5 – 6 kg.
Food: krill, fish
Breeding grounds: Macquarie Islands

The royal penguin has a slate-grey upper side and is white on the sides of its head, on its chin, neck, throat and on its underside.
The chicks look similar, but are grey-brown in colour and the feathers on the crown are yellow rather than the adult orange. They are closely related to the macaroni penguin, but are slightly larger.

They breed mainly on Macquarie Island, an Australian protectorate around 1450 km southeast of Hobart in Tasmania. However, breeding pairs have also been discovered on the Falkland Islands.

Their newly-laid eggs can be spotted between September and November. Around the middle of the Australian winter they disappear for a good four months. At this time, they migrate to more northerly waters, but we are still unsure about precisely where they go for the winter months and at precisely what point they leave the Macquarie Islands.

Scientific classification of this penguin is still a little unclear, and some experts tend to describe the royal penguin as merely a colour variant of the macaroni penguin. Others are of the opinion that both types of penguin should be accorded the status of species.

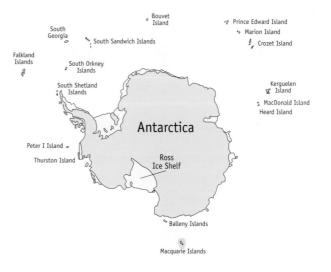

Photos: Kerstin Hinze

Snares Penguin

Genus: *Eudyptes*
Species: *Eudyptes robustus*
Population: circa 33,000 pairs.
Status: stable
Height: circa 51 – 62 cm.
Weight: 3 – 4 kg.
Food: crabs, fish
Breeding grounds: Snares Island

The snares penguin breeds exclusively on this island which is one of a group about 200 km south of New Zealand. This island is a whopping 250 hectares in size (620 acres).

The snares penguin is slimmer and a little taller than its northern relation, the royal penguin. The missing stripe on its cheek and its rather darker plumage set it apart.

Because this group has such an isolated breeding area, the snares are certainly fairly safe from the intrusion of man. From May to August Snares won't in fact be seen on the island where they breed, but at sea. They are said to roost on the lower branches of small trees, where available, on Snares Island.

Outside of the breeding season, the snares penguin is also to be found on neighbouring islands which are often several hundred kilometres away.

The foundation of the rookery begins with fierce territorial battles.

In September or October the female lays two eggs, four or five days apart. The little chicks hatch after about four weeks but, almost always, one or other of the chicks dies: it falls out of the nest or starves to death. The young birds begin to form larger groups after about a month, and moult after around 75 days as they develop towards sea-going independence.

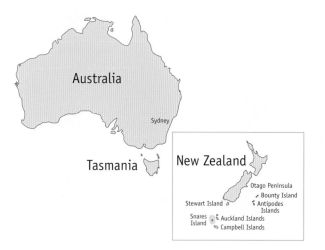

Photos: Joseph Van Os

Rockhopper Penguin

Genus: *Eudyptes*

Species: *Eudyptes chrysocome (crestatus)*

Population: circa three million pairs

Status: stable

Height: circa 47 – 60 cm.

Weight: 2.4 – 4.2 kg.

Food: krill, fish

Breeding grounds: in the sub-Antarctic circum-polar region and islands in the southern Indian Ocean and the Atlantic.

The rockhopper penguin is blue-grey and slate-black on its head, chin and gullet. Its underside is white and it has slate-black wings. Its bill is short and powerful, its colour varying from orange to reddish. It hops on land with its feet kept tightly together and is recognised as the 'mountaineer' among penguins.

The rockhopper gets its name because the rookeries are often to be found on rocky, inaccessible coasts. The penguins themselves get there by jumping.

Rockhoppers lay two eggs and protect them aggressively. They will even attack humans quite fiercely. These are the smallest of the crested penguins and are the least temperature-sensitive. For this reason they have the widest distribution of all crested penguins.

They exist in three sub-species and spend the April to September period at sea.

There are around three million rockhopper penguin pairs. The males come to the Falkland Islands at the start of October and the females follow on about ten days later. In the first weeks of November, the females begin to lay their eggs. At this stage, food is mainly squid, lobster krill and fish. Rockhoppers breed in the Falklands in some 35 or so different rookeries and are the most prevalent penguins of these islands.

Photos: Winfried Wisniewski

Fiordland Penguin

Genus: *Eudyptes*
Species: *Eudyptes pachyrhynchus*
Population: circa 1,000 to 10,000 pairs.
Status: endangered
Height: circa 50 – 71 cm.
Weight: 3.0 – 4.9 kg
Food: fish, especially squid
Breeding grounds: New Zealand's South Island and offshore islands.

Fiordland pengins look almost the same as rockhoppers, but without the extended feathers on their crowns and the plumage behind the yellow stripe on the side of their heads does not droop down. Their wings have a narrow white fringe on the inside edge of their upper sides. The sides of their throats are often flecked with white. The young birds look similar, but are greyish and white around the gullet and chin.

On land, they hop or run in with a rather clumsy gait, and very little is known about their seasonal movements. They live in the waters around New Zealand and in winter they probably migrate as far as the Chatham Islands, southern Australia and Tasmania.

Fiordland penguins can be found in their breeding grounds between July and March, and they leave them between March and July each year.

They seem to be rather secretive penguins, breeding in the thick vegetation of the rainforests and among large ferns.

Because they are so elusive, it is very difficult to make accurate estimates of the total population. It is thought that there are only between 5,000 and 10,000 pairs, but the real figure may be much lower. Numbers have undoubtedly fallen greatly since 1900.

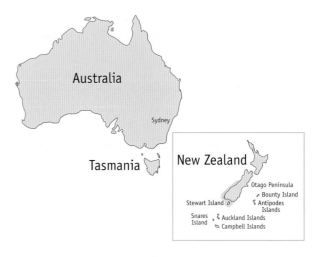

Photos: Joseph Van Os

Erect-crested Penguin

Genus: *Eudyptes*
Species: *Eudyptes sclateri*
Population: between 200,000 and one million pairs.
Status: endangered
Height: 55 – 69 cm.
Weight: 3 – 7 kg.
Food: squid, crabs
Breeding grounds: South Pacific.

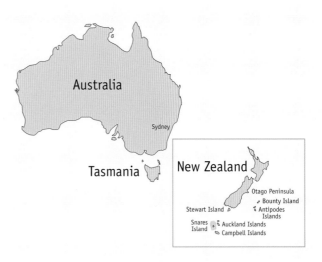

The erect-crested penguin has similarities to the fiordland penguin, but is larger. Two rows of feathers form white stripes on the inside edge of its wings. You can tell it apart from the rockhopper penguin on account of its height.

Erect-crested penguins breed in the sub-Antarctic climate in their rookeries during winter and are at sea from around May to September. Not much is known about their migration patterns during these times.

They have similar patterns of behaviour to the fiordland penguin, but are in fact less aggressive. They are the only species among the crested penguins which can raise up their decorative feathers. They are to be found south of New Zealand in the ocean, but sometimes also as far afield as New Zealand itself, Victoria and the Chatham Islands. Occasionally they breed on Bounty Island, the Antipodes and on the Aukland Islands.

Sometimes this species makes and appearance on the Falkland Islands too.

The breeding season of the erect-crested penguin begins around September and is accompanied by rather fierce territorial battles which are fought, of course, over the best nesting sites. The erect-crested penguin builds its nest from stones, twigs and grass. The female lays her two eggs here.

The first egg is usually the smaller one, and is often not incubated at all. If it is, then the chick usually dies immediately after birth.

Related species are the fiordland penguin *(Euryptes pachyrhynchus)*, the snares penguin *(Eudyptes robustus)*, royal penguin *(Eudyptes schlegeli)*, macaroni penguin *(Eudyptes chrysolophus)* and the rockhopper penguin *(Eudyptes chryosome)*.

Yellow-eyed Penguin

Genus: *Megadyptes*
Species: *Megadyptes antipodes*
Population: circa 1400 – 1600 pairs.
Status: endangered
Height: circa 55 – 77 cm.
Weight: 5.7 – 8.5 kg.
Food: fish
Breeding grounds: Forests along the coasts of New Zealand's South Island and offshore islands

The yellow-eyed penguin is slate-grey on its upper side and blackish on its head. The chicks have a yellow band on the sides of their heads only.

These are unusual characters in the penguin family since they like to brood alone.
When they do join a rookery, then they always keep a wide distance from their neighbours.

The yellow-eyed penguin differs conspicuously from both the royal penguin and macaroni penguin because of the light yellow marking on its head, which is very wide across the forehead and does not end in protruding feathers.

This large penguin has the smallest breeding population of all penguin species and is probably, as a result, the most endangered.

Unlike other species, the yellow-eyed penguin stays in its breeding colony or on its breeding site the whole year round.

The species has suffered massively as a direct result of deforestation in the dense coastal areas which are its breeding grounds.

From the 1950s onwards, destruction of the forests has reduced the population by some 75 per cent.

While many other penguin species are closely related to one another, the yellow-eyed penguin stands separate and alone – and highly endangered.

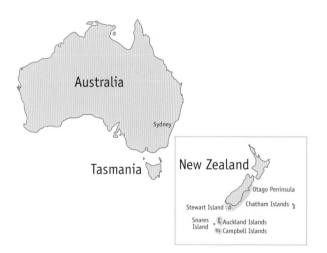

Photos: Kerstin Hinze

Little Blue Penguin

Genus: *Eudyptula*
Species: *Eudyptula minor*
Population: circa 500,000 pairs.
Status: stable
Height: circa 40 – 46 cm.
Weight: 0.9 – 1.5 kg.
Food: small fish
Breeding grounds: South coast of Australia, New Zealand, and islands in the surrounding areas.

The little blue penguin is actually blue-grey. The sides of its chest and its face are ashen coloured, and its underside is white. The chicks look similar.

It is the smallest of all penguins, and weighs just one kilogram.

The little blue penguin shuffles about on land in a strange, wave-shaped motion with its body tilted forward. On the coasts of Australia it is the only common penguin of this small size and simple colouring.

It does not tend to travel far from its breeding site and will remain fairly close to it throughout the year. The pairs remain loyal, often spending many years together on the same breeding site.

They incubate in hollows which they make with their own feet and bills when needs must. The little blue penguin is closely related to a sub-species of the New Zealand white-flippered penguin. They exist in six sub-species. Ninety-five per cent of the population breeds in Australia and the remaining five per cent in New Zealand.

Their habitat often lies along busy shipping routes and near conurbations. As a result, the little blue penguin is a frequent victim of oil slicks and other pollution, and of coastal fishing.

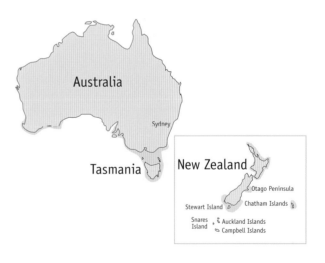

Photos: Opposite page: Kerstin Hinze. Above: Winfried Wisniewski.

Enemies and Neighbours

Penguins do not need to fear polar bears or arctic foxes since these potential predators have not made it to the Antarctic and penguins have not reached the Arctic. The enchanting photo of the 'polar bear with penguin' can only be produced with the aid of a computer.

In the Antarctic at least, penguins do not have any large predators to fear on land, but all the same, there are more enemies and neighbours than the penguin would ideally like in its environment.

In and under the water they are threatened by large predatory fish and sharks, by fur seals, sea lions and sea leopards.

On land the threat comes from skuas, sheath bills, giant fulmars, seagulls and in some breeding areas from imported animals such as cats, rats and mice. Their presence encourages harriers such as caracaras who will exploit the opportunity of easy prey.

Above: Mollymawk albatross with its young in a typical 'pot-nest'. It is a neighbour but not an enemy.

Opposite page: Penguins often emerge from the sea wounded. It is uncertain whether this king penguin will survive its injury. The wound to its upper body will lead to severe loss of blood.

The weaker predators mainly steal dead chicks or unguarded eggs. Large and strong predators such as skuas and caracaras go for eggs and young penguins. The adult penguins are in most danger when they are in the water, where sea leopards and orcas lurk. Fur seals are a danger for the Australian little blue penguin and the penguin species of the South American coast are hunted by sea lions.

The impact of predators on penguin numbers and the development of rookeries is, on balance, not particularly great. The propagation of the rookeries is more directly affected by the availability of ice-free breeding grounds and by whether or not climatic conditions are favourable during the breeding season. Seen from this perspective, global warming could lead to an increase in the number of breeding sites.

Top: Here, a caracara on the Falkland Islands has caught a penguin, killed it, and is now eating it.

Bottom: The sheath bill ('white as snow' in Greek) usually takes on the role of scavenger in a penguin rookery, but sometimes it also eats eggs and whole chicks.

Top: The giant fulmar also belongs in the enemy category. It is both predator and scavenger, with the distinction between the two being a fluid one. In the barren biotope where the Antarctic penguin rookeries are, a predator must be flexible and there is often no strict differentiation between the two types.

Bottom: The skua is also an enemy of the penguins, but it also preys on fish which swim near the surface, and probably lives almost exclusively on this fare during the southern winters. The skua eats eggs as well as dead chicks, but is perfectly capable of killing penguin chicks for itself. Skua pairs sometimes divide large penguin rookeries between themselves so that each pair as a strictly circumscribed hunting ground.

Opposite page, top: The migratory albatross is a neighbour to the penguin rookeries. Shown here on South Georgia.

Opposite page, bottom: Here, a blackish cinclodes (tussac bird) is examining the body of a Southern Elephant Seal for parasites on Sealion Island in the Falkland Islands.

Top: A breeding colony of the black-browed albatross on the Falkland Islands.

Bottom: Geese on the coast of Argentina are among the penguins' neighbours.

Overleaf: Neighbours in the water include whales, marine iguanas, turtles and mantas, depending on the penguin's habitat.

Penguins and People

Throughout history, humans have always had a certain soft-spot for penguins, perhaps because their waiterly appearance and upright way of slightly ungainly walking make them so different from other types of bird.

We have not, though, actually ever really been particularly kind to them. Even as early as the 15th century, when they were first discovered by crews on European ships, we took away their eggs and served them for breakfast, lunch and dinner. Thousands, if not millions of them, were burned or pickled on ships.

Penguins are very easy to catch on land, and so provided an inexhaustible supply of fresh meat for these early researchers and seamen. The killing of penguins was too much even for the captains of some ships. One captain noted in his diary: "it is difficult to keep the men from their indiscriminate killing. I give an order that only birds with good plumage should be killed, and that this should then be taken care of. But it makes little difference. You have hardly turned your back for one moment when these men

Previous page: On land, fur seals often live near to penguin rookeries. Here you can see a large rookery of king penguins on South Georgia in the background.

Opposite page: An emperor penguin with chick.

Above: Penguins can live perfectly comfortably in the Antarctic. Humans, on the other hand, need to take certain precautions to protect their skin, if they want to survive out here for more than a day. *Photo: Joseph Van Os.*

continue to beat every living creature within their reach to pulp, as many as they can catch."

On the other hand, evolution has been extremely kind to the penguin over a very long period of time. They have existed for around 60 million years, and for virtually all of this time they have been safe from us because we have only been troubling the Antarctic for about the last 500 years.

For 59 million, 999,500 years, penguins were able to live relatively peacefully and unmolested in the Antarctic and sub-Antarctic, without oil slicks to daub their feathers and to cause death by hypothermia; without drift nets to catch and drown them in and without humans to kill and then burn or eat them in the hulls of their ships.

It is a source of great personal regret to me that the great auk has become extinct in the seas of the north. In the southern oceans too, we have lost so many interesting species of penguin.

It is we who must be held accountable for the fate of the great auk. Practically all were slain by humans.

The extinction of most of the other lost penguin species is down to evolution. Above all, I would have loved to have seen the giant penguin Pachydyptes ponderosus out in the wild: a penguin of almost two metres in height and weighing 135 kg must have been an incredibly impressive and fascinating creature to behold.

Today, admittedly, penguins are no longer killed directly by humans, but the 3,000 inhabitants of the research stations and the 10,000 tourists certainly have an impact, and unsettle the creatures.

This page: The animals of the Antarctic are not easily impressed by humans, whether tourists with cameras or locals – like here on the Falkland Islands – who simply want to watch the birds incubating.

It is difficult to say which is the most or the least damaging: Is it the ships with tourists, which only ever stay for a short time at individual locations, perhaps half a day at one rookery and up to a week in the vicinity, or is it the 40 permanent winter stations and the ever increasing number of summer stations, which are permanently occupied, with their associated waste and their chemicals?

Human civilisation is becoming increasingly sensitive to the environment and our responsibilities for its protection in general. The Antarctic and its wildlife are finally getting more thoughtful attention, and that gives us hope for the future.

Perhaps, in 500 years, the penguins will have it every bit as good as they did during the nearly 60 million previous years when they were undisturbed by us.

Top left: Oil spills, accidental or otherwise, can cause immense suffering and distress for penguins.

Top right: Whoever wants to observe little emperor penguins must visit before the Antarctic spring, before the ships are able to sail in, and must come equipped with tents.

Bottom: Researchers, mountaineers and nature photographers come to the Antarctic in planes like this during the Antarctic winter when ice stops the ships sailing here.

Penguins and Photography

Penguins are amenable photographic subjects. They don't fly away, they don't usually make any sudden movements, they are easy to photograph because they do not hide in thickets, you don't have to hunt for them and they are always very photogenic. There is just one problem: It requires quite an effort to reach them, and the shipping lanes in these regions are often rather choppy. You have to stoop down and lie on the floor. There are also lighting problems because there are no mid-tones, at least not in the Antarctic and the Antarctic Peninsula.

But in principle it is simple and enjoyable. You take a lens with a medium focal length, from 100 to 300 mm, and you're pretty much ready for anything. Add a wide-angle for panoramic pictures of the rookeries and your toolbox is complete.

It only becomes irksome when you've set your heart on getting that perfect shot of a cute little emperor penguin chick on its parent's feet. Then things can get exasperating.

You can of course take photographs of all types of penguin, their breeding colonies and their young in the pleasant Antarctic spring and summer. But for emperor penguin babies, alas, you have to come a few months earlier, when it is very cold, very windy, when the days are short and the ships cannot sail yet because of the ice.

Then you can't sleep in a comfortable cabin and tuck into the delicacies which the ship's cook has prepared. Instead you have to fly in in a tiny aircraft, sleep in tents at temperatures down to minus 20 or 30 degrees Celsius, and probably the less said about the quality of the cuisine the better!

A tip: The most beautiful final destination for penguin photos is South Georgia in the Antarctic spring in January or February. It is simply dreamlike at this time of year, and one of the most beautiful places on earth because of the penguins, but not for that reason alone.

Bibliography

W.B. Alexander
Die Vögel der Meere
Paul Parey, Hamburg, 1959

lan J. Strange
Wildlife of the Falkland Islands
HarperCollins; London, 1962

Wayne Lynch
Penguins of the World
Firefly Books, Willowdale, 1997

Boris Culik
Pinguine – Tessloff Verlag, 1998

Kevin Schafer
Pinguin Land – Tecklenborg Verlag, 2001

www.anjaspinguine.de, 2005

Niels Carstensen
Pinguine – Ellert & Richter, 2002

Dietland & Christine Müller-Schwarze
Piguine – A.Ziemsen Verlag,
Wittenberg Lutherstadt, 1977

Lloyd Spencer Davis & Martin Renner
Penguins
T & A D Poyser, London 2003

Opposite page: The author in front of his hotel room on the Dawson-Lambton Glacier close to an emperor penguin rookery. *Photo: David Tipling.*

Top: Penguin photography – Florida it ain't.

Bottom: Because you can hardly find a 'mean grey tone', which nature photographers usually use for calibration, here you have to use a light meter (not an exposure meter).

Other books in the *Wildlife Monograph* series

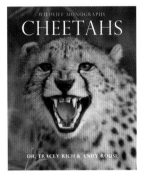

Wildlife Monographs –
Cheetahs

ISBN: 1-901268-09-8

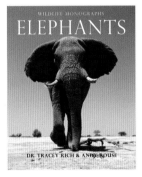

Wildlife Monographs –
Elephants

ISBN: 1-901268-08-X

Wildlife Monographs –
Giant Pandas

ISBN: 1-901268-13-6

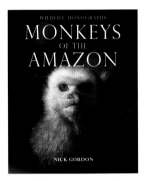

Wildlife Monographs –
Monkeys of the Amazon

ISBN: 1-901268-10-1

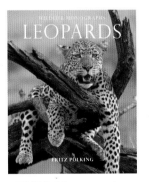

Wildlife Monographs –
Leopards

ISBN: 1-901268-12-8

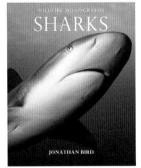

Wildlife Monographs –
Sharks

ISBN: 1-901268-11-X

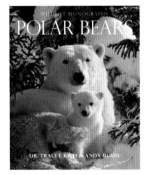

Wildlife Monographs –
Polar Bears

ISBN: 1-901268-15-2

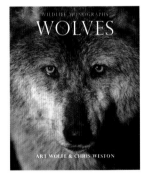

Wildlife Monographs –
Wolves

ISBN: 1-901268-18-7
     978-1-901268-18-8